What We Harvest

What We Harvest

Poems by

Frank C. Modica

Cover design by Shay Culligan

ISBN: 978-1-63980-026-1

Kelsay Books
502 South 1040 East, A-119
American Fork, Utah 84003
Kelsaybooks.com

I dedicate this chapbook to my maternal grandfather, Calogero (Charlie) Saccaro. His quiet sacrifices almost a century ago made this book possible.

Acknowledgments

I am grateful to the editors of the following journals in which these poems first appeared, some in an earlier form or with a different title.

Adelaide Magazine: "Man Up," "Drift," "Blurring the Lie"

Beyond Words Literary Magazine: "Dream Garden"

Bindweed Magazine: "Odyssey"

Cacti Fur: "Grandpa's Death Watch," "My Father's Name"

Green Hills Literary Lantern: "1965"

Literary Yard: "The Shovel Man"

Rat's Ass Review: "Cross-stitch"

Sin Fronteras: "Becoming the Writer"

Soft Cartel: "Déjà Vu," "Skyward"

Spindrift: "12 Flags," "Bedpan Blues"

Steel Toe Review: "Baker's Dozen"

Terror House Magazine: "War Games"

The Pangolin Review: "First Funeral"

The Tishman Review: "Falling, Falling," "The Flood"

The Write Launch: "Circulation," "Shall We Gather at the River?"

Tipton Poetry Journal: "Palimpsest"

Versewrights: "Transubstantiation," "Matinees," "Background Noise," "Blood on the Wheels"

Contents

Becoming the Writer

after a line by W. H. Auden

Sicily beat down my grandfathers,
starved them, cursed them,
pushed them off the island.

They came to America stuffed
into the third-class quarters
of the *Perugia* and the *San Giovanni*.

Promised *streets paved with gold* by shipping agents,
they lived in tightly packed tenements,
travelled down mean brick alleyways.

Francesco toiled in steelyards, glass factories,
Calogero sold bootleg wine to feed his family.
No room for poetry on the South Side of Chicago—

They didn't rhapsodize about Sicily or America,
wove family tales over plates of pasta, glasses of wine,
carved the stories into the hearts of *la famiglia.*

But the grandfathers died years ago,
the aunts and uncles dispersed to the suburbs,
and family memories untold slowly evaporated.

Everyday I try to pull memories from old photographs
and bits and pieces of family lore to write these stories
on plain white paper, backlit laptop keyboards.

Sicily and America hurt them into my poems.

12 Flags

Sicily tossed him
into the belly of a tramp steamer.
Italy forgot about him,
the green, white and red
tricolor wasn't his flag.
Grandpa carried a lonely
banner on his back, a tattered shirt,
as he sailed across the
Mediterranean to America.

Navigating the great corn
deserts of the Midwest,
he arrived in Chicago,
married a widow,
a neighborhood girl.
Often out of work, he sold
homemade wine in Bronzeville.
His sons and daughters stayed
in those closed streets,
raised families in the city,
but his grandsons, granddaughters
went to college, got educations,
moved away from the old neighborhood,
became teachers, programmers,
business owners, accountants.

At Christmas dinners
the family gathers together
to eat ravioli, pierogies,
sushi, barbacoa, kreplach.
On his granddaughter's
refrigerator a photo of his
children, grandchildren,
and great-grandchildren;

12 flags, 13 languages,
English, German, Japanese,
Yiddish, Italian, Spanish, French,
two African dialects, Swedish,
Russian, Polish, Vietnamese;
His DNA woven into
A quilt of many colors.

The Shovel Man

after the poem by Carl Sandburg

Every summer Grandpa worked magic
in his backyard garden with a shovel in hand.
He loved spading dirt over newly seeded beds,
setting poles for string beans, sharing the bounty

with his family. In his youth, he was always
tilling farm fields with a battered shovel
to pay his monthly tithe to the Church in Sicily,
scraps left for him, the only healthy people he saw

were priests and monks. He fled to America
because he was starving, he had no future.
In Chicago, more grinding poverty.
He became *a shovel man, a dago*

building a railroad overpass, a story
he never shared with his grandchildren.
On weekly trips to Grandpa's place
my brother and I passed under the tons

of dirt, rock and concrete, his monument.
Grandma told us how Grandpa helped build it.
We'd enter a long dark tunnel, smell the damp,
feel the cold oppression of the freight trains

and trucks over our heads. We feared those
weekly eclipses, sighed with relief every time
we came out at the end into the sunshine, laughed
because we didn't have to shoulder his shovel.

Bedpan Blues

When Uncle Joe
visited Grandpa's
hospital room,
he found an empty bed,
sheets disheveled,
dinner still sitting on a tray.
Frantic, Joe dashed
down the hallway, shouting,
"Where's my father?"
A quick search
found him behind the
door in the bathroom,
one hand clasping
that damn IV pole
with its dangling tubes
and hanging bags
and beeping machines,
the other hand holding up
his white hospital gown.
"I don't want no damn bedpan."

Grandpa's Death Watch

Grandma and Grandpa
inhabited their tenement
like two foreign countries.
Grandma cooked and
cleaned in the kitchen,

Grandpa lounged in his
smoker's chair wedged behind
the dining room table.
They slept in separate bedrooms,
framed pictures of Jesus

leaned back-to-back on the
wall between them. For
fifty years they kneaded
their secrets into loaves
of tall, crusty bread,

hid them behind white
porcelain shaving mugs.
"Charlie was not my first love,"
Grandma whispered to me
as I drove her to the hospital.

Transubstantiation

Perfect half-moon floured shapes sit
on an immaculate white sheet to dry,
ravioli aligned in perfect rows and columns,
their doughy edges crimped with a fork,
four perfect holes poked in the top—
ready for the boiling water,
ready for the red tomato sauce,
ready to be consumed.
But they are almost too beautiful to eat,
too perfect to pass from fork to mouth.

Augustine prayed before his conversion,
"Make me chaste, but not yet."

In her kitchen Grandma measured
the flour in handfuls of this,
the salt and parsley in pinches of that,
working alone without a written recipe;
hours of work to transform
the mundane into the sacred.
No one violated her sanctuary,
no one decrypted the culinary secrets
passed down mother to daughter for generations
in Sicily and carried over to L'Merica.

She hoarded this knowledge
until one Saturday her daughters,
unnerved by the prospect of
Grandma's mortality and
the possible loss of the treasury,
descended on her kitchen
with measuring cups, spoons,
paper and pencils to
pry open the tabernacle.

Grandma was reluctant
to give up her secrets,
but the daughters pinched the salt,
measured her handfuls of flour.
They squeezed the balls of elastic dough,
trying to quantify the textures
of too much, not enough, not yet,
rechecking measurements, rewriting notes
for this communion, this family tradition.

When Grandma finished her ravioli,
she was done, the secrets written down
for other cooks, other dinners;
she never made them
after that afternoon.
The daughters, not yet ready
in Grandma's eyes,
took the recipe home.

Dominus Vobiscum

Old women dressed in housecoats
sit or kneel together in wooden pews,
cotton scarves cover their grey heads.
They mumble responses to
familiar Latin invocations,
finger plastic rosary beads,
clutch faux leather missals
as they wait for the sacred meal.
Smoke rises in the sanctuary
from wax candles on the altar,
votive candles gutter and
flicker in the shadows.
In their hearts the women sing,
"Oh let this Holy Communion
bind us together with unbreakable cords,
let our children come and rise with us
to hymns of eternal glory."

Their grandsons and granddaughters
commune together in faux leather booths
under the flickering faux candles
of an Olive Garden Italian restaurant.
They sit shoulder to shoulder,
ghost reflections flicker off their faces.
Everyone folds their hands over cellphones,
thumbs fingering their own salutations.
One diner rises, texts a cab without
breaking the silence, "Let there be
a clean cab on cold, clear streets."
Another texts his brothers and sisters,
"Let our parents and grandparents
run and not grow weary, eat and not faint,
let them rise and never fall alone."

Falling, Falling

Dad towered over
us like Prometheus.
With a burning cigarette
at his lips he seemed to
carry fire down from the
heavens as he exhaled long,
wispy tendrils of smoke.

Mike and I stood entranced
as the white clouds rose
in the air, beckoning
us with visions of majestic,
mysterious mountains.
Wanting a taste of his magic,
we pleaded, "Can we try it?"

Thinking perhaps to teach
us a lesson, he held
the unfiltered cigarettes
up to our young lips.
We swallowed those
first puffs; our initiation
tarnished and tempered
by fits of violent vomiting.
Mike and I looked at dad,
our eyes bloodshot and teary.
The fires scorched and burned,
and a god fell from the heavens.

First Funeral

I sat in the backseat
of an old Mercury sedan
with my brother Mike
while Mom paid
her respects.
Dad stayed with us;
we were too little
to walk through
the funeral home,
to see the dead body
of a stranger
in an open casket.
To pass the time
Dad leaned over
the front seat of the car,
told Mike and me stories
about Frankenstein,
the Wolfman, and Dracula.

At first Mike and I
shrieked with delight
while we huddled together,
delighted with the special
attention from Dad,
but as the yellow
street lights
cast long shadows
on the threadbare upholstery,
as we peered through
the fog-shrouded windows,
saw dark shadows
surround our car,
we begged Dad to stop,
cried for Mom to come back.

1965

That was the year Sister Marie
published my first poem
in a school newsletter,

a dream fantasy about a wild jungle.
I can still smell the mimeograph toner,
feel the smudged sheets of white paper.

That spring I rode my first bicycle,
learning how to stop with the coaster brake
instead of running into telephone poles.

That summer I bought a paperback edition of
Robert Frost poems at a Ben Franklin dime store.
The store clerk followed me around

until I paid for the book. I carried it in my backpack,
hid it from my friends. That fall I waved at old women
in babushkas sweeping the sidewalks.

They never looked up, never waved back.
That winter I learned about fences,
how I wasn't their good neighbor.

Last Lunch

I crawl under the wood desk,
rest my head on khaki knees.

A bell rings in the hall,
Sister Marie tells us

to pray for peace.
I fold my hands,

stare out the window,
wondering if I'll see

the Soviet missiles fall from
Cuba. Barbara Jean cries,

my stomach rumbles. Will I make it
home before the mushroom clouds bloom?

War Games

Enemies were easier to identify
playing war games with my brother.
Stalking the South Side alleys
and back streets, we waged war against
the German and Japanese soldiers
who battled our uncles and neighbors.

When playmates joined us
we took turns as the Americans
or the enemies.
We'd shoot them with our toy guns,
they'd shoot us—
we'd clutch our chests,
writhe on the ground,
get up, dust off our jeans,
ready for more battles.

Playing war was much easier
before fetid jungles,
body bags,
before Ia Drang,
Khe Sanh,
Tet.

Man Up

Good Catholic boys in button down shirts
and blue jeans fought on the school playground,

rising and falling in the masculinity standings.
This brutal competition snared everyone,

large and small, Polish, Italian,
or Irish, and my turn was coming.

I tried everything to dodge this bullet,
but holy cards and rosaries didn't save me,

good grades couldn't defer the inevitable;
I had to meet the bullies in the alley after school.

If I didn't fight back I was already a loser,
my adversaries would stalk me in the stairways,

shove my head against a wall, call me a fag.
I had to show up, suck it up, be a man,

so I put my glasses in a book bag,
took a punch, threw a punch.

Bloody nose, black eye,
so what, Italian boys don't cry.

Matinees

Every Saturday Mike and I
walked to the Ramova,
a second-run movie house
to watch double features,
cartoons, coming attractions.
We trekked down hot, gritty

city streets in the summer,
tramped through snow
all winter, always stopping
to read comic books
at corner newsstands.
Walking home after the shows

we acted out action scenes,
driving chariots around
the Hippodrome or chasing
Japanese Zeroes across
the skies of Guadalcanal.
When we moved out of the city

we went to Saturday matinees
at two suburban theaters.
The owners doubled the ticket prices,
dropped the double features.
In high school Mike went out
for football, I joined the wrestling team.

I got good grades, he got suspended
for smoking in the boy's restroom.
I went to college, he barely finished
high school. Sometimes we'd go to
a movie and try to catch up with each
other. After he died I returned

to the old neighborhood. National
chains replaced most of the local
stores along Halsted. The Ramova
stood shuttered and shattered,
its battered marquee
gap-toothed and rusty.

Drift

I borrow my father's powder blue
1966 Chevrolet Bel Air 4-Door Sedan, an unsexy vehicle
but big enough to transport six testosterone-addled
teenage boys to a rock concert.

I drive to Rockford, a 90-minute trip
from suburban Chicago to the indoor stadium,
parse the minutes for the warm-up bands, REO Speedwagon,
hope nothing upsets my timetable.

I dismiss the weather reports—it'll blow by, just a dusting,
but the concert starts late, the warm-up bands drag on.
I watch the clock—*we're cutting it close,*
hear murmurs through the crowd—*a big storm's on the way.*

After the first song of the headline band
I hustle my buddies out of the auditorium.
A freezing slush accumulates on the local roads,
the car feels unsteady at every stop and turn.

By the time we hit the interstate big snowflakes
plaster the windshield; a blowing, howling mess.
I wish away the truck stop phone call to my parents,
count the hours until I face the music.

Dream Garden

I think about my Dad all the time,
so many words I wanted to say
before he died, it's no surprise he pops up
in my dream garden like ubiquitous dandelions
who are so brilliant before their transformation.
I accept his appearance from the grave
without anger or dismay even though
he offers unsolicited advice again,
sentences that spin around my sleep
like spring and summer puff balls;
they explode with whirling motions
when you barely breathe on them,
unlike silent Lazarus, newly raised from the dead,
who needed help to unwrap the linen shrouds
binding his head and mouth,
whose words go unrecorded.

I only knew my late wife Marci four years.
She kept most of her opinions
to herself in our short time together.
I don't know what would have happened
if we had more years in our relationship,
but we shared good words, soothing words
the night before she died, no regrets
to wake me up from my dreams.
It's no surprise she shows up
only once or twice a year
in the uncultivated yard of my mind,
passes through my sleep
like the end of Elijah's dream;
a quiet whisper

at the edge of the garden,
no earthquake or hurricane
to disturb me, just wild blue flax
faded before I knew it bloomed.

Ghost Bike

I edge up to a left turning lane
as the street lights shimmer through

my slush-splattered windshield.
When the stop light turns red

I notice a white bicycle chained
to a street pole—tires flat,

pedals halted in mid stroke,
a shrine to a dead bicyclist.

The bike brings me back
to Dad's visitation that afternoon

as I rehash the pungent
phrases I'd left unsaid.

I turn on a FM classical station,
hum along with Aida,

one of his favorite operas.
I have his records and CDs,

wish I'd listened along with him.
He worried about my bike riding,

felt I took too many chances.
We never rode bikes together.

When the left turn arrow flashes
I turn off the radio, wish

I was riding a white bicycle
instead of looking at one.

My Father's Name

after Kay Ryan

He spoke Italian
before he spoke English.

At home his family
called him Francesco,

but in kindergarten
the teacher called him Frank.

He was Frank
when I was Frankie.

I became Frank in high school,
during heart surgery he became a free man.

On his birth certificate: Francesco—
On his death certificate: Frank.

Odyssey

He trekked three hours
to his dad's house, his duty,

driving him to the hospital
for bypass surgery.

In the hospital for 9 hours,
he walked loops around the

brightly lit corridors, prayed
with the rest of the family.

Feeling like a boat tossed
about in the wake of a storm,

he raged against the gods,
besieged the nurse's station.

He drove back home to rest,
waited for news. At the tenth hour,

a phone call—the blood sacrifice
on a surgical table. No mercy.

Baker's Dozen

Every year on my brother's birthday,
I reminisce alone in a city of people
who do not know his name.

I look at family albums, his twisty smile.
He is flour and water rolled into pastry dough,
one last piece of pie left on the table.

Circulation

He opens the front door
to let in fresh air as
lightning flashes fracture
the dark tree-shadowed lawn.

Fifty years rumble through
his memory, echoing long
thoughts about his brother.
He liked this kind of weather.

Thunder rattles through
the screens of open windows,
daring him to close them.
A late storm batters

the shingled roof,
blows his angry
words across the porch.
Moths flare up

against the porch light
seeking refuge. Tired after
grieving his brother, he closes
the door, locks the windows.

Background Noise

A garbage truck rumbles
down the street like
rolling thunder. He
sleepwalks out of the

bedroom, stumbles into
the kitchen. Half-empty
wine glasses glare at him
from the table. Morning

shadows envelop every
room—silent, accusatory.
Heat shimmers from the
slanted garage roof tiles like

an exhausted lover. He
hears a car door open, waits
for a knock at the front door,
doesn't know if he'll answer it.

Blurring the Lie

I claim I've gazed at women's faces,
arms, legs, buttocks, breasts
because I admired their classical proportions,
their undeniable beauty.
I loudly assert that I've never acted like

the creepy guys who sit down uninvited
at women's tables and hit on them,
who think they are God's gift to every lady.
But can I be honest with myself,
re-evaluate all my interactions,

make amends for all the times
I was the arrogant jerk
leering at women who walked down the street,
who stared down the fronts of their dresses,
who looked away only when they caught my eyes?

Cross-stitch

During the day she positioned children
in wheelchairs, changed diapers,
tube-fed kids in a public school
special education classroom.

She loved her job.
During the night she worked
as a stripper at a local club
down the street from the school,

the buses passed it every day.
One afternoon she told
the other teacher aides
that she used to slash her arms

with a razor blade,
watched them bleed,
though she didn't do it anymore.
She wore long sleeves

never talked to the teacher
about the scars that glared under
the shadows of her shirts.
And I didn't ask.

Shall We Gather at the River?

The plastic hospital curtain
segregated our miseries
like a reluctant stream.
On my side of the deluge
I lay in bed, testing the waters.

My roommate waded
wraith-like around the divider,
skeletal legs protruding
under his hospital gown.
He looked past me

through the window toward
the forest preserves across the street.
His speaker phone jack-hammered
against the beige shoals
of our sterile fraternity

like a pneumatic drill against
river pilings as he raged against
the nurses and the hospital,
"Look for my body on the
banks of the Des Plaines River."

This wasn't the baptism
I was seeking, the resurrection
I aspired to. Wanting to escape,
I beseeched the nurses,
"I fear the flood that's coming."

The Flood

Years ago I drove by the levee
of Old Shawneetown.
Cruising down the pot-holed,
abandoned streets,
past glass-shattered storefronts
and eyeless, tooth-gapped houses,
I rode uptown and saw
the flood stains etched high
on the tall Corinthian columns
of the Old National Bank.

Some townspeople tried to save
their memories, raising up
levees of earth and clay
to hold back the waters,
but most of the residents
packed up their dreams
and moved to higher ground.

Years later I saw on the news,
 pictures of a new and greater flood-
the Ohio River cresting
at Old Shawneetown,
a river swollen by days of rain
rising two feet over flood stage.

Levees and dikes weren't enough
to hold back the deluge as the river
surged in a 100-year flood,
breaching dams, scouring
old towns and bottom lands,
mocking the great walls of America.

Blood on the Wheels

He might have seen
the cat darting across the street,
or maybe it was his children
crying out from the back seat,
"Stop the car, stop the car."
But he felt the thump
under his wheels,
he heard the yowling screams.
The children sobbed,
"Help the kitty, Daddy."
He pulled off to the side of
road, watched the cat
through his open side window,
saw the blood on the street.
The cat writhed in pain,
paws scratching the sky,
but he had places to go,
it was already too late,
he didn't want to mess up
the car seats and mat.
He put the minivan in gear,
drove away, but his children's
accusations tore at his heart,
"You killed the kitty."

Years later driving alone on
the interstate in a different car
he saw the dog, or was it
a coyote? It dashed across
the median on a collision
course with his car.
He tried to slow down
but couldn't stop in the traffic,
couldn't safely swing away.

He heard the sickening thud,
felt in his hands the crushed bones.
He didn't see the animal in his
rearview mirror, there weren't
any children crying
in the back seat of the car,
but he knew there would be blood.

Night Ranger

I finish the
last bedtime story.
All the children
have finally fallen asleep.
I go into the living room,

plop down on the couch,
alone in a quiet house.
My wife works nights,
she always works nights.
I turn on MTV.

As the music starts,
I pick up my air guitar,
strum a few power chords.
The lead singer sings
about his lost love,

I launch into a perfect
air solo, note for note
sing along with the band,
"When you close your eyes,
do you dream about me?"

Skyward

My daughter bounces
on the swing seat under
the leaf-mottled sunshine
of an Illinois park. Her short
legs pump the warm spring air.

The rasp of the swing bolts
screeches like red-tailed hawks
chasing dreams across the sky,
the gusting wind scatters
our dancing shadows.

When I push her up to the clouds
we both reach up for memories,
but gravity pulls us earthward,
too soon the moment passes;
our thoughts touch the cool ground.

Walking back to the car,
she grabs my hand,
laces her fingers in mine.
Looking up in my eyes, she asks,
"Daddy, can we swing again?"

What Do You Remember?

The morning after her fourth birthday party
my youngest daughter
opens the refrigerator expecting her prize.
When she finds an empty shelf
she asks, "Dad, where's my cupcake?"

I shrug, display empty hands,
mutter under my breath,
"It's just a stupid Hostess cupcake."
She cries, I bluster, offer up
lame excuses instead of her treat.

As I back away from the refrigerator,
I don't stop to consider what I have lost.
I stand half in and half out of the kitchen,
teaching her dishonesty in my silence
while she tries to teach me love.

Déjà Vu

Sitting in a restaurant,
I hold my red-headed
three-month old granddaughter,
look into her steel-grey eyes.
She laughs at my silliness,
watches an overhead fan;
swish-swash.

As I gaze at one future in my hands,
my attention wanders a lifetime,
out the restaurant windows,
into a graying January street,
where sharp winds rattle
the winter-shredded trees...

until my granddaughter
laughs again, catches my eye,
reels me back into the moment
then looks over my head;
swish-swash.

Palimpsest

Suppose you
tattooed your life
on broad stretches
of arm, back,
stomach, thigh—
intricate pictures,
of your deeds
good and bad,
hoping to pass
on the stories
to your children.

After your death
will the family
keep those tales
and gather every year,
dragging out your carcass
to retell them—

or will they scrape off
those old tattoos
and stencil their own
truths and lies?

About the Author

Frank C. Modica is a cancer survivor and retired teacher who taught children with special needs for over 34 years. His writing is animated by interests in history, geography, and sociology. Frank's short story "Homemade" was selected as an Honorable Mention in the Midway Journal 2017-1000 Below Flash Prose and Poetry contest. His poem "Rainbow Bus" was the 2017 Champaign-Urbana Metropolitan Transit District Poem Contest winner and was featured on all the local buses for a month. His work is forthcoming or has appeared in Beyond Words Literary Magazine, Frost Meadow Review, Green Ink Poetry, Blue Mountain Review, and Raconteur Review. "What We Harvest" is Frank's first published chapbook.

Frank grew up with a deep respect for his ethnic roots in the dense urban neighborhoods on the South Side and the western suburbs of Chicago. He now lives in Urbana, Illinois.